How Sprinkle the Pig
Escaped the River of Tears

Anne Westcott and C. C. Alicia Hu

Illustrated by Ching-Pang Kuo

Jessica Kingsley Publishers
London and Philadelphia

First published in 2018
by Jessica Kingsley Publishers
73 Collier Street
London N1 9BE, UK
and
400 Market Street, Suite 400
Philadelphia, PA 19106, USA

www.jkp.com

Library of Congress Cataloging in Publication Data
A CIP catalog record for this book is available from the
Library of Congress

British Library Cataloguing in Publication Data
A CIP catalogue record for this book is available from
the British Library

ISBN 978 1 78592 769 0
eISBN 978 1 78450 670 4

Printed and bound by Ashford Colour Press Ltd

books in the same series

Bomji and Spotty's Frightening Adventure
A Story About How to Recover
From a Scary Experience
ISBN 978 1 78592 770 6
eISBN 978 1 78450 670 4

How Little Coyote Found His Secret Strength
A Story About How to Get Through Hard Times
ISBN 978 1 78592 771 3
eISBN 978 1 78450 671 1

Introduction

The body possesses innate capacities to ensure we make it through distressing situations. This inborn wisdom of the body inspired me to develop Sensorimotor Psychotherapy^{SM} (SP) decades ago. I have made it my life's work to elucidate this largely untapped resource so that we can engage it to help ourselves and others heal from severe stress, trauma, and attachment disruption.

The Hidden Strengths Therapeutic Children's Books series captures this essential spirit and intention of Sensorimotor Psychotherapy^{SM}. The authors render the core concepts of this approach accessible to both caregivers and young people struggling in the aftermath of overwhelming experiences. The stories do so with sensitivity and particular attention to illustrating the bodily experience of the child in an engaging and compelling manner.

Understanding the language of the body helps us make sense of the often confusing behaviors following trauma and separation from loved ones. We freeze, run away, collapse, fight, hide, cry for someone bigger and wiser to help us, and even dissociate or do things we wouldn't normally do, like steal, to make it through. These instinctive bodily survival defenses are automatically engaged in times of threat. Each of us employs the defensive response(s) that will work best in a particular moment given the immediate circumstances, so there is no single best survival strategy. These compelling stories emphasize the hidden strengths in the characters' survival behaviors, staying true to the foundational principle of SP that the physical actions taken are the person's best attempt to respond to the situation they face.

Over time, we develop habits of defensive responses, often repeatedly engaging just one or two survival defenses. These then become our default behaviors in the face of subsequent threats, which is compassionately and wisely illustrated by the appealing characters in the stories in the series. Anyone helping children will find new ways to look at the often challenging and misunderstood behaviors children display after stress. The stories also encourage caregivers and children to become curious about the survival functions these behaviors may serve.

As the authors, both trained in Sensorimotor Psychotherapy^{SM}, describe how the characters adapt to challenging circumstances, the body's wisdom is revealed. Each character favors a different survival defense, which is cleverly portrayed through the character's movement, posture, and physiology. The pictures and rich descriptive text convey the real-life bodily and emotional experience of so many children, without evaluation, judgement, or interpretation. The stories describe events and behaviors from each character's viewpoint, offering a variety of perspectives. Doing so enhances understanding of how the body responds and influences the meaning we make of what we see, hear, and feel. The ability to gain perspective, to stay curious, and to experiment are core to Sensorimotor Psychotherapy^{SM} and woven into each story. Children will feel relieved and understood as they recognize themselves and their peers in the myriad struggles of the characters. Behaviors children might have perceived as ineffective or worse, a confirmation of their own badness, may very well be transformed into a strength that can be adapted to help them thrive. Our bodies adapt via movement, posture, and physiology.

The supplements following the stories will help caregivers recognize the signs of these survival strengths in the simple body clues of gesture, posture, tone of voice, facial expression, eye gaze, and movement. This is what I have termed the "somatic narrative" core to Sensorimotor Psychotherapy^{SM}. When one understands the language the body uses to tell the story of distress, puzzling and confusing behaviors by children begin to make more sense. When we can make sense of our children's behaviors, we are better equipped to respond in flexible and sensitive ways to help our children feel better in their bodies, hearts, and minds.

Pat Ogden, Founder, Sensorimotor Psychotherapy Institute, 2017

About the Hidden Strengths Series

This book is part of a series for children who have lived through extremely stressful times. The series is inspired by Sensorimotor Psychotherapy^{SM}, a unique approach to trauma treatment developed by Dr. Pat Ogden. The series is designed to present children's distress in a realistic yet digestible way.

The authors have carefully crafted the stories so as to reduce sensory stimulus and not overwhelm traumatized children. You will notice this in the language chosen: simple yet descriptive, in a way that seeks to highlight hidden strengths in potentially shaming moments. You will also see this in the images as they shift away from bright color to grays at particularly tense moments. The very crafting of the book was guided by the principles and knowledge of Sensorimotor Psychotherapy^{SM} and the authors' deep understanding of children. This attention to the reader's experience makes the book useful to anyone caring for traumatized children.

We possess many kinds of strengths to get through challenging times. Some are obvious and some are harder to see. Many of these hidden strengths live in our bodies and leap to our rescue instantly, bypassing our thinking. These strengths try to keep us safe in times of danger when we have to act fast and may not have help around.

These books will help you and your child gain understanding and appreciation for the amazing abilities that live inside of you. By sharing these stories with your child, these books will help them to reduce feelings of shame, recognize that problematic feelings and behaviors can be a response to stressful times, and feel better in their body.

OTHER BOOKS IN THE SERIES

You and your child will meet several characters over and over again when you explore the series. The animals' lives intertwine in unexpected ways. Gaining a deeper window into each character changes our feelings toward the animals. The series is crafted to generate curiosity, empathy, and perspective-taking in the reader. These capacities are stunted by trauma and chronic stress.

READING TIPS

Find a space where you are both in a relaxed and playful mood. Allow 20–30 minutes to explore and talk about the content.

1. Allow children to decide the reading speed. Some children enjoy exploring the details in pictures more than the storyline. Some children may have emotional reactions to the content and want to skip or fast-forward to a later part of the story.

2. Children are very creative. Your child may ask questions you can't answer. Support your child's curiosity by encouraging them to come up with their own answers.

3. Suggested activities are provided at the end of each book. They are designed to help deepen the learning from the story through all your child's senses.

Not long ago, Sprinkle the Pig had lived with the big pigs, Koko and Juju. They took care of Sprinkle in a cozy little home next to a field of golden daisies.

But one day Sprinkle had to leave Koko and Juju. Sprinkle had to move far away to a different family.

Now Sprinkle lives in a rambling old farmhouse at the edge of the forest.

Here, the trees looked odd, the air smelled strange, the house seemed sooo big. Even the wind sounded different.

He felt like he had landed on a different planet.

Soon it was time for Sprinkle's first day at his new school near his new home. Sprinkle was nervous but also curious.

His belly was fluttering like a balloon full of butterflies. His mouth was dry like the bark of a tree. His cheeks were hot like two tomatoes in a sizzling pan.

Sprinkle saw his teacher and classmates. A little boy rabbit and a little girl cat were making a model airplane together. He thought, "I hope they will play with me."

The teacher said gently, "Welcome! We've been looking forward to meeting you. I am Teacher Owl."

Then, Teacher Owl introduced Sprinkle to the boy rabbit, Bomji, and the girl cat, Spotty.

The fluttering in his stomach slowed when Sprinkle heard Teacher Owl's soft voice. Feeling a bit calmer, Sprinkle began to peek around at his classmates. "Will Bomji and Spotty like me?" he thought. "Will they sit with me at lunch?"

At lunch, Sprinkle saw his chance to make friends. He rushed over to Bomji and Spotty, calling, "Hi! Can I sit with you?"

But he was so nervous and his feet ran so fast that he tripped. With a thump, Sprinkle bashed headlong into Bomji's tummy.

Before Sprinkle could open his mouth to say sorry, Bomji exploded like a volcano and yelled like hot lava in Sprinkle's face. Sprinkle became very small. His mind froze, and all of a sudden he found it hard to breathe.

Sprinkle's heart began to pound like a drum, louder and louder.

Frightened, he ran away from the school, faster and faster.

He ran and ran, all the way to the edge of town.

After a while, Sprinkle began to tire. His legs became so heavy like lead.

As he slowed, his eyes felt hot and they stung. His throat began to squeeze tight. Nothing could get out.

Deep in the valley, Sprinkle slumped on a damp log. As Sprinkle curled up, he felt the tightness in his throat, and a deep feeling of missing home which spread in his heart.

Memories of Koko and Juju bubbled up. Sprinkle remembered how his Koko used to give him big hugs. Deep in his body he felt an urge to snuggle up to her. His arms ached for her now.

Poor Sprinkle needed his Koko and Juju's cuddles. When he remembered they were far, far away, he let out a cross grunt. He was mad. "This isn't fair!" he squealed, but no one was there to answer him.

Tears started rolling down Sprinkle's cheeks, and he began to cry out loud. The more he cried, the harder it became to stop...

Sprinkle's tears seemed endless. They poured out of him, filling the valley floor. The tears rose up to Sprinkle's middle, but try as he might, he could not stop crying. Soon, his tears became a river!

Still crying, Sprinkle grabbed hold of the log as the river of tears whisked him downstream.

The current grew fierce, tossing poor Sprinkle this way and that. Sprinkle cried out for his Koko and Juju. His ears filled with the pounding of his heart; his eyes clouded with tears.

Through his tears, he could barely make out a monkey on the riverbank reaching out to help, but he was too far away.

Poor Sprinkle's strength was fading, and he could feel his grip slipping. Sprinkle's heart sank.

But then he heard the monkey's firm voice: "Trust the current of the water, it will carry you to me." Sprinkle's body relaxed a little, and soon he felt the river bottom beneath him. He heard the gentle whisper from the monkey: "It's okay, you are safe now."

Poor Sprinkle was so worn out, he collapsed on the soft grass by the river. The monkey was careful not to startle him, but just settled patiently nearby as Sprinkle rested.

The monkey knew to watch over Sprinkle. The monkey's body would talk to Sprinkle without words. His regular breath would send calmness to Sprinkle's tired body.

The last tears rolled down from Sprinkle's eyes. His body became heavy and soft. Sprinkle snuggled deeper into the grass as the gentle breeze caressed his back.

As he rested, a sweet buttery scent filled Sprinkle's noise. Sniff~ Sniff~

The smell of daisies brought a lovely hidden memory back to Sprinkle.

His hoof felt a gentle squeeze, and a warm tingling started to flow up his leg and into his heart.

Sprinkle was remembering holding his Koko's hoof as they walked through the field of daisies back home.

As the sun dried his skin, he felt a big itch. He rolled on his back and began to wiggle, trying to scratch that itch.

Then, he remembered how his Juju would tickle him and he began to giggle.

A memory bubbled up in Sprinkle's heart of how he and Juju use to play chase and wrestle!

After a big game of wrestle, Sprinkle always felt hungry.

Juju would have a big bowl of sweet crunchy carrots ready.

Sprinkle remembered munch, munch, munching. He could almost taste their sweet, juicy crunching.

With his tummy all full, Sprinkle loved best to curl up on Juju's big belly.

Sprinkle and Juju would doze together. Juju would snore, and with each snore Sprinkle would rise gently up and down. The steady hum made Sprinkle feel safe and warm.

A tune twinkled in Sprinkle's ears; he remembered bedtime with Koko. Every night, she would sing him a lullaby as he drifted off to sleep.

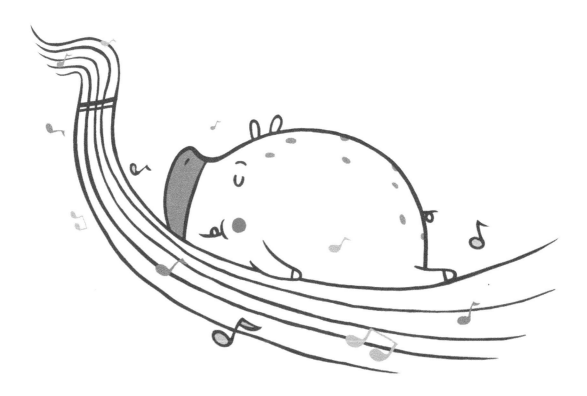

A short while later, the soft breeze woke Sprinkle. His body was cozy now, and filled with memories of his Koko and Juju.

Remembering Koko and Juju seemed to feed his whole little pig body with love and belonging.

Sprinkle's fear faded. As his strength returned, he became curious. He slowly began to look around.

Sprinkle was surprised to see the monkey gazing at him. A bit startled, he asked, "Who are you? Where did you come from?"

The monkey answered, "I saw you travelling down the river of tears. I tried to reach you but you entered the rapids."

"Ohhhh, was that your voice I heard?" Sprinkle started to remember. "I was so scared when I lost my grip on the log, but your words gave me courage."

The monkey smiled. "You seem calmer and more settled now."

Sprinkle nodded shyly, "Thank you!"

The monkey added, "Pigs need to be very brave to face and feel such big feelings. When feelings can flow through us like the river, they can ease our hurts and bring warmth and hope back to our hearts."

Sprinkle let out a long sigh. He took a breath in and thought, "I made it."

Sprinkle still felt lonely, but now he also felt hopeful. He knew Koko and Juju's love was a hidden strength within. The loving memories lived like a life raft inside his body, supporting him when the water became rough. All he needed to do was to use his five senses to bring them back.

With this new-found courage, Sprinkle looked back toward school.

Holding a daisy in his hoof, Sprinkle said to himself, "Maybe tomorrow I could say sorry to Bomji for bumping into him, and ask him if he would like to share my carrot?"

Let's Talk About Sprinkle's Tears and Hidden Strengths

Remember how Sprinkle was upset after Bomji yelled at him? We all feel sad and upset when someone is rude to us, but Sprinkle's upset was so much bigger than normal because he was apart from Koko and Juju. His upset got even bigger when he became frightened in the rapids. These emotions cause us to cry out very loud for help. Asking for help is a strength that lives in our bodies. If you were Sprinkle crying alone in the valley, what would you want from people who care for you?

Sometimes, we are sad because we cannot live with the people we love. We may even cry and get angry. Sprinkle does not live with Koko and Juju right now. What do you think happened?

Play Time

BUILD A COZY PIGGY HOME FOR SPRINKLE

1. Try building or drawing a cozy piggy home for Sprinkle. You can use simple things: pillows, blankets, even under a table can work.

2. What would you like to put inside this cozy piggy home? Choose things you think will help Sprinkle to feel comfortable and good in his body.

3. What can you do to soothe Sprinkle in this cozy piggy home? Sing a song? Pet Sprinkle's back? Tell Sprinkle a story?

AFTER THE GAME: MAKE YOUR OWN COMFORT PACKAGE

Make a special comfort package with your parent to help you feel safe.

PARENT TIPS

Work with your child to make a special bag. Choose a bag or a box for the comfort package. Put objects in that make your child think of you. *Suggestions:* picture, recording of your voice, shirt that smells like you, a special stone.

Help your child to discover and choose what brings him/her comfort. *Suggestions:* there is no limit here. Have your child use their five senses to find what feels good.

Guide for Grown-Ups

NEW VOCABULARY AND STORY GUIDE

This story is about a sweet little pig who has a bad moment at school and becomes very upset. His upset is so large he almost drowns in his strong emotions. Often, adults mistake strong emotions like these for tantrums and bad behavior. Hidden in the story is the knowledge that when we are separated from loved ones we are more vulnerable to upset. The story also reveals the hidden strengths we all possess to get through this upset.

page 14

HIDDEN STRENGTH: CRYING OUT FOR HELP

On the surface, one may think Sprinkle cried because Bomji yelled at him. However, the story reveals how Sprinkle cried out for help in two special ways that live in our bodies:

- **Cry for help demanding a loved one:** When yelled at, Sprinkle ran away and he found himself all alone. He started missing Koko and Juju. He cried out for them in anger because he needed their comfort and they were not there!

- **Cry for help to survive:** Then, as the tears started to turn into a river, Sprinkle faced the real danger of drowning. This survival threat triggered an even louder and more desperate cry. This cry is a survival defense called the attachment cry. The attachment cry is a primal animal defense like fight, flight, freeze, and submission. It is the deep cry a child makes in the dark from overwhelming need and fear.

page 15

HIDDEN STRENGTH: THE BOND OF CONNECTION TO A LOVED ONE

The bond of attachment is like good medicine for the body. Once formed, it lives inside of us and we can call it up just by remembering. When something triggers us to remember our loved one, like a smell, the sound of a voice, or a picture of them, our whole body goes through a change. It is like the sun breaking through the clouds. The world looks a little better; you feel a little brighter. Mother Nature built our bodies with this remarkable ability to make good chemicals just by remembering loved ones. It is very handy to be able to bathe yourself in warmth, security, and goodness when you need it.

page 13

HIDDEN STRENGTH: ACCESSING COMFORT
THROUGH OUR FIVE SENSES

Remembering our loved ones is not just about thinking of them, it's about bringing back the sense of safety, warmth, and fun in different parts of our bodies. Sprinkle the Pig's hoof warmed up when the smell of daisies brought back the memory of holding Koko's hoof. This warmth soothed his hoof, so cold from the chilly river.

page 21

When Sprinkle scratched his itch by wiggling, the back and forth movement brought back memories of wrestling with his Juju. The body movement also loosened the stiffness in his limbs from holding onto the log for so long. The warm sensations in his hoofs and the greater flexibility in his body worked to calm Sprinkle's nerves after the intensity of the rapids.

HIDDEN STRENGTH: COURAGE TO RIDE
THE BIG EMOTIONAL RAPIDS

We are built to feel powerful emotions. This ability is part of how we all handle big overwhelming events. Our bodies and minds heal from upset quickest if we are able to let big feelings flow through us like the river. However, just like Sprinkle, children can find these emotions to be too much, so they need a kind adult's help. The support of another can make it possible to ride the rapids of emotion, just like the monkey's presence helped Sprinkle.

page 30

Sprinkle gained confidence by riding the strong rapids of feeling that hit him. With a caring adult's steady presence, children grow the ability to handle powerful feelings. They may need to ride the rapids of emotion over and over again. Feelings of mastery and self-confidence grow with each trip. This confidence will help Sprinkle as he continues to be apart from Koko and Juju. It will also help him meet the challenge of making new friends and adjusting to a new school.

LET'S LEARN ABOUT ATTACHMENT

In this story, we learned that when a child feels upset or frightened, the child's "attachment system" turns up very loud. Here is some important vocabulary to help you understand the many meanings in Sprinkle's tears.

ATTACHMENT

Like all mammals, we are born with the urge to connect to others of our own kind. Attachment is the closeness bond that is forged and strengthened when the caring adult reliably attends to the child and their needs. Humans need attachment to live just as we need water to live. This attachment bond provides us with the hidden strength and security necessary to go out and explore the world with confidence and resilience.

page 24

Here are some ways to strengthen the attachment bond in your daily life: making eye contact back and forth between child and adult; touch contact; rocking; holding; verbal playful call and response; shared curiosity and exploration; providing simple repetitive routines and simple resources like tasty food, clothing, and companionship; showing support when the child is facing challenges; spending time listening and sharing stories of happiness as well as complaints; listening to music or reading books in the same space; even sharing chores together; celebrating a child's growth, such as walking, picking up their room, cutting vegetables safely, or learning a new song.

ATTACHMENT SYSTEM

Our body and mind include many parts; for example, our arms can reach out, hug, and hold on to loved ones; our feelings inside get warm and soft when we feel their closeness; our mind holds

page 25

pictures and thoughts of loved ones inside; our skin knows the touch of our special loved ones.

The attachment system is like the train conductor inside us. This conductor gets our mind, feelings, and body to work together to build close bonds with trustworthy people who also want to build bonds with us. When we face stress and danger, our "attachment system conductor" is very smart; it tells us to seek closeness, comfort, and protection from a loved one.

ATTACHMENT PROTEST AND ATTACHMENT CRY

Attachment protest is the discontent and frustration children express when they don't get the comfort they need from their caregivers. The child cries out, expecting that a caring person—a parent, teacher, older sibling, or other adult—will show up and help them to feel better. When that loved one does not come or is not available, children will protest in stronger ways. They could kick, bite, scream, or throw things. Older children may pull away, refuse to talk, or use mean words.

Attachment cry is an animal defense common to all mammals. Human children rely on older people for their survival because they are born with more growing to do after birth than any other animal. They will not survive without care, so they instinctively cry out when in real danger to draw help to them.

The intense feelings that accompany attachment protest and survival cry can easily overwhelm a child, preventing them from recognizing and being comforted by our presence. Sitting with a child in this kind of intense distress can overwhelm adults who offer comfort. We may feel frustrated that the child can't seem to let us help them. We can become angry or annoyed at the child. At other times, we may feel helpless and ineffective in our efforts, so we give up or pull away. It's even common to feel like the child is being manipulative.

We are better able to sit back and wait in the face of the emotional storms in our child when we recognize this emotional intensity as one way children's bodies respond to danger and separation from loved ones.

HOW TO SOOTHE ATTACHMENT PROTEST

In this story, the old monkey understands attachment protest. That is why he waited patiently for Sprinkle, without adding too many words or trying to soothe Sprinkle with physical touch too soon. He understood not to get too close too fast. He understood to go slowly and take time. He also knew that intense emotions naturally quiet over time, just as the rapids gave way to the calmer current.

page 29

The old monkey used his own stable breathing to provide a calm, rhythmic presence. This helped Sprinkle's nerves to calm down. As Sprinkle settled, his mind, body, and feelings began to work together. We see Sprinkle begin to recall his attachment figures through his senses: the smell of daisies, the warmth in his hoof, wiggling and remembering wrestling.

TENDING THE GARDEN OF SECURE ATTACHMENT

Little ones relax in their caregivers' arms when their touch feels safe and secure. When feeling loved and comforted, children's bodies relax; often it feels like they melt into the support of the other. Their bellies soften; emotions can flow. Older children and adults may need guidance to learn how to trust support and let go in their bodies. Some ways to teach our bodies in this important capacity include practicing yoga, qigong, dance, and massage. Sometimes, special help may be needed from a professional.

page 27

When parents are not available, children could get comfort from objects that remind them of loved ones, such as a blanket that smells and feels of home, a stuffed animal, a favorite toy, or a song their loved one sang. Even a heavy blanket covering the child's back may mimic the safe feeling of being hugged and protected. When children are able to fully take in these objects through their senses, their bodies remember the nurturing and soothing from loved ones. Over time, these memories can become positive body resources available when needed. This ability is what we call internalized secure attachment.

Anne Westcott's life work focuses on helping people (young and old) who have been having a hard time to understand how their bodies give them hidden strengths. She is a clinical social worker and psychotherapist who lives in Concord, Massachusetts with her husband and two daughters, and she loves to be outside and moving, no matter what the weather.

Growing up with manga (comics) in Taiwan, **C. C. Alicia Hu** knows the secret of learning new things is to look at words and pictures together. That's why she enjoys making stories like this series! As a practicing psychologist in Moscow, Idaho and Pullman, Washington, she also enjoys using simple body exercises to help people feel better about themselves.

BOMJI AND SPOTTY'S FRIGHTENING ADVENTURE

A Story About How to Recover from a Scary Experience

One sunny day, Bomji the Rabbit and his friend Spotty the Cat meet something very scary while picking flowers in the woods.

The friends manage to escape, but afterward Bomji just doesn't feel safe anymore. His body feels a bit different and he starts to have bad dreams. His friend Spotty is worried about Bomji – how can her friend be helped? Luckily, wise Teacher Owl is there for them.

This therapeutic picture book allows children and adults to talk about a frightening experience. The story is followed by helpful guidance for adults on how to help your child. It explores how your body and how you feel are affected by scary experiences, and explains how you can use your body to help to recover too.

BOMJI AND SPOTTY'S FRIGHTENING ADVENTURE

A Story About How to Recover from a Scary Experience

Anna Westcott and C. C. Alicia Hu

Introduced by Pat Ogden

Illustrated by Ching-Pang Kuo

HOW LITTLE COYOTE FOUND HIS SECRET STRENGTH
**A Story About How to
Get Through Hard Times**

In a deep dark forest, Little Coyote grows up
with tough gang of big strong coyotes. They are
cruel, call him names, and order him about all
day long.

Little Coyote is too small to run away or to
stand up for himself, so he learns to do what
he's told and makes his body small so nobody
notices him. Then, one day he goes on an
adventure and ends up discovering new hidden
strengths that he never knew he had.

This therapeutic picture book is written to
help children aged 4–10 and adults to talk about
difficult experiences growing up (including things
they may still be going through), and explores
how they can affect how your body feels and
reacts to things. It is followed by easy to read
advice for adults on how to help your child.